Out of Sight, Out of Mind

A Writer's Guide to Mastering Viewpoint

Out of Sight, Out of Mind

A Writer's Guide to Mastering Viewpoint

by

Ken Pelham

Cover Art and Design: Jennifer Pelham

Cover Imagery Source: Nicola Perantoni

Cover Typefaces:
Bebas Neue by Dharma Type
Braeside by Typodermic Fonts Inc.

ISBN-13: 978-0-9895950-3-2

Acknowledgments

Thanks are in order to the members of the Maitland Writers Group, to all the writers who've attended my viewpoint lectures, and to the libraries and staff who've graciously allowed me the use of their facilities in which to make these presentations. The feedback received helped sharpen this guidebook. Most of all, many thanks to Amy and Jennifer, and my wife, Laura, for their help, support, and critiques.

—kp

Table of Contents

PART I: Understanding Point of View........1

Viewpoint Matters..........................…....…..3

Types of Viewpoint...........…....................…5

First-Person..6

First-Person Ancillary...........................7

First-Person Multiple..............................9

Viewpoint Within Nested Stories...............10

The Camera in First-Person......................11

First-Person Plural...............................11

Second-Person.....................................12

Third-Person......................................13

Third-Person Subjective.................….....…..14

Third-Person Limited...........................…...15

Trumbo's Third-Person Limited Experiment..16

Third-Person Objective.........................…17

Third-Person Omniscient........................…18

Multiple Third-Person Subjective vs. Third-Person Omniscient...............................…...19

Third Person "Deep"....…......................…20

Third-Person Plural..............................…..22

PART II: Writing in Viewpoint.........23

Choosing Point of View....................25

Viewpoint in Nonfiction....................27

Do Not Disturb...............................29

What a Character Knows (or Doesn't)...29

Dialogue......................................31

How a Character Sees Others..............33

Seeing One's Self...........................34

Mind-Readers................................37

Show, Don't Tell............................39

Viewpoint Changes in Third-Person......41

Head-Hoppers................................42

Be True to the Character....................43

Mixing and Matching Viewpoints.........47

Closing Arguments..........................52

About the Author...........................57

PART I

Understanding Point of View

Viewpoint Matters

Among the community of readers, writers, agents, editors, and publishers, you frequently hear about viewpoint. An editor will tell the writer his work has viewpoint errors, or has consistent viewpoint, maybe even creative use of viewpoint.

When your editor criticizes or praises your point of view, she's not talking about your personal views on politics, religion, music, or sports. Probably not, anyway. She's referring instead to the mechanics in how the story is conveyed from the characters' points of view.

A few years back, I participated as a judge in a literary awards competition. After reading a number of entries submitted by writers at widely differing skill and experience levels, I noticed that what hurt new writers the most was point of view. I also noticed that writers with skill and experience, yet few publication credits, were making some of the same mistakes, although with less frequency, as the new writers. The thing seems simple, yet is rife with pitfalls, some glaring, some subtle.

When the leader of our local writers group asked me if I could give a presentation on any topic that our members would find useful, I knew right away that I wanted to talk about viewpoint mistakes. I've since given that presentation a

3

number of times, and it evolved into this guidebook.

We all read books in which the narrative flows along quite nicely, and suddenly a line or paragraph goes *clunk!* I'm a slow reader to begin with, often because I might reread lines several times. I certainly reread it when it goes *clunk!* Grammatical errors are frequently the culprits, those things which are clumsy or just flat-out wrong. But if the grammar is perfect, what causes the *clunk*?

Too often, point of view mistakes.

I've tried to boil the rules down to the essentials. We'll begin with basic definitions and explanations of the types of viewpoint, followed by creative use of viewpoint in genres, and finally, recognizing, avoiding, and fixing all viewpoint errors, great and small.

By the way, the terms "viewpoint" and "point of view" are interchangeable. In our shorthand world, point of view frequently sneaks about as just "POV." This guidebook will use all three. Other writers sometimes use additional shorthand, like "TPO" for third-person objective, but I'm not crazy about that.

Types of Viewpoint

On this planet, there exist three basic literary points of view. I do not know how the terms were achieved, and they make little sense to me as labels. However, they are the conventions and we must live with them. You recall them from high school. I hope. They are:

- First-person.
- Second-person.
- Third-person.

That's it. I've wracked my brain to invent a fourth-person point of view, and have failed to do so.

Only three to work with? Your creativity hog-tied? The good news is, each of these three points of view possess variations and forms.

Nearly all modern fiction is written in either first-person or third-person. We'll cover those in depth, for good reason, and go into second-person just for the hell of it.

A key thing to remember is that the story may be told as if the viewpoint character is unaware that he or she has a reading or listening audience, watching his or her every move, invading his or her thoughts. It's one of the great talents with which we, as readers, are endowed. We own this ability to suspend disbelief and hop aboard for the ride.

First-Person

First-person viewpoint is told as if from a fully participating narrator. "Narrator" is just that, the character, real or fictional, telling the story. In first-person, the viewpoint character is expressed as "I", "me," or "myself." The forms "my" and "mine" follow.

First-person may be written as though the narrator is intentionally writing or orally communicating her story with the audience. Like she's delivering or writing her last testament in her jail cell.

First-person is not limited to "persons" of the human variety. A story can be narrated by a rat character... and frequently has. Your big toe can be a first-person narrator, but readers may be reluctant to buy a copy of that story.

Right out of the gate, first-person has an obvious advantage of immediacy and intimacy. The author can write the actual thoughts going on in the narrator's mind. If the narrator thinks, *I hate cats*, the author can write it exactly that way.

That advantage, we will see, is not always what the skillful writer wants.

In first-person, the story's main character is usually the narrator, as in **John D. MacDonald's** Travis McGee series. McGee narrates his own exploits, solves his own problems, worries about his own boat. Making him both narrator and main character works well. This is sometimes called **first-person protagonist**, and it's the wise choice for that series, and probably for most.

But not all, as in **first-person ancillary**.

First-Person Ancillary

Consider the Sherlock Holmes stories, by **Arthur Conan Doyle**. Holmes is without question the main character and protagonist of the stories. However, the narrator is Holmes's sidekick, the capable Dr. Watson. Why?

The first-person advantage of immediacy and internal thoughts and emotions would have countered what Doyle sought to portray in Holmes. He envisioned Holmes as a brilliant, enigmatic sort, with a mind most of us can't begin to fathom. It made little sense to place the reader inside Holmes's mind, as it would spoil the illusion of aloof, untouchable brilliance. Rather, we catch glimpses of him at work as dutifully reported by Watson.

This viewpoint mode is called **first-person ancillary**. The narrator is not the main guy. Important as Watson might be, he's ancillary to the great Holmes.

Admittedly, Holmes frequently describes in long passages to Watson whatever adventure he has recently gotten through. Although told as dialogue, these passages function as first-person narratives in themselves. This kind of viewpoint shift to another first-person narrator is called **temporary first-person.** It can come off as a clumsy effort, so pains should be taken to ensure that the shift (for the reader) sails along effortlessly.

Another shining example of first-person ancillary is **F. Scott Fitzgerald's** *The Great Gatsby*. Nick Carraway serves up the narration, although the story clearly revolves around Jay Gatsby and his great, unattainable love, Daisy Buchanan. The choice of Nick as the viewpoint character makes this novel succeed. Fitzgerald wanted us to have Gatsby only revealed in bits and pieces, with Nick's opinions of the principal characters evolving the more he learns:

> *...he stretched out his arms toward the dark water in a curious way, and, far as I was from him, I could have sworn he was trembling. Involuntarily I glanced seaward—and distinguished nothing except a single green light, minute and faraway, that might have been the end of a dock. When I looked once more for Gatsby he had vanished, and I was alone again in the unquiet darkness.*

First-Person Multiple

First-person multiple sounds like a mistake. If first-person is told by *the* narrator, how can there be more than one? What gives?

Simple. There are just more than one narrator. Each of them gets a turn at the wheel.

A structural problem with first-person multiple becomes readily apparent. In third-person, you can—with care and skill—switch viewpoint characters within a single scene. If you attempted this with first-person multiple, you would most likely leave the reader confused and disoriented. If first-person multiple is to be used, it should be done with a complete change of scene, and preferably not within the same chapter.

Bram Stoker pulled it off with a clever approach in *Dracula*. The novel is told in the form of letters, journal entries, ship's logs, telegrams, newspaper clippings, and doctor's notes, by multiple characters, almost all written in the first-person.

Dracula begins as scribbled in the journal of Jonathan Harker, the young English businessman summoned to remote Transylvania to assist the mysterious Count with his planned expatriation to London. From there, we shift to the logbook of a doomed ship's captain, the letters of Mina Harker, Jon's fiancé, Mina's friend Lucy

Westenra, (who's way hotter than Mina, but that's beside the point), and of course the medical journals of Van Helsing.

A novel such as *Dracula*, written as a series of documents, is called an **epistolary** novel (from the Greek, *a pistol, Larry?*). Epistolary stories don't have to be first-person, by the way. They can be told through third-person accounts in newspaper or magazine clippings, as in **Stephen King's** *Carrie*.

Gillian Flynn weaves a more restricted first-person multiple narrative in *Gone Girl*. The central structure and strength of the story is the "he-said/she-said" back and forth between husband and wife narratives.

Viewpoint within Nested Stories

Variations on first-person multiple can be built around stories that are **"nested"** within another story. Some are structured such that there might be a first-person narrator telling the story of another first-person narrator. As an example, in *The Time Machine*, by **H.G. Wells**, the story opens as narrated by a guest summoned to the home of a friend. The friend (identified by the narrator only as "the Time Traveler") tells the first-person account of his adventure into the distant future. As he concludes his tale, we shift back into the first-person viewpoint of the original narrator.

The Camera in First-Person

In photography and film, because there is an actual camera involved, there is a defined and limiting point of view. The camera *cannot* enter the mind, despite what a director or photographer might claim. However, in so-called point of view filming, shot as though a character is filming something—a film within a film—the intended effect is that of first-person. Or as when the camera shows what the director wants you to believe is exactly what this or that character is seeing. This little trick comes off as somewhat clumsy and unconvincing, and has become a cliché in horror movies, often accompanied by heavy breathing. After a gory scene, the camera usually shifts out of this and back into normal objective mode.

Multiple first-person in motion pictures seems to have been achieved to a degree in the cinematic equivalent of first-person prose, in the recent trend of "found footage" movies. Stuff like *The Blair Witch Project*, *Cloverfield*, and *Europa Report*. Don't get me started.

First-Person Plural

First-person plural is the cousin of first-person multiple. The cousin you lock in the attic and never let out. The story is told by a narrator... but the narrator is not an "I," "me," or "myself."

11

It's the plural "we," "us," or "ourselves." It's first-person, but as if told by more than one person. "We" becomes the narrator.

Caution! Don't try this at home, kids. If it sounds unusual, well, it is. It can be quite unwieldy, heaving about as if a group is telling the story. It has the tone and feel more of a political speech than a story.

However, in the hands of a talented writer, it can come alive and just seem like the right choice. A terrific example is "A Rose for Emily", a short story by **William Faulkner**. In this haunting story, the little town itself becomes the narrator, a sort of collective consciousness as well as a collective conscience. The reader even feels a bit of vicarious guilt, as we all have known and watched and ignored someone like Emily in our lives. And it works:

> *We did not say she was crazy then. We believed she had to do that. We remembered all the young men her father had driven away, and we knew that with nothing left, she would have to cling to that which had robbed her, as people will.*

Second-Person

In a **second-person narrative**, "you" become the narrator. It's rarely used, and for good reason: it has a weird, almost out-of-body feel to it. It can easily come off as a cheesy, overwrought attempt at forcing emotion. Kind of comic-bookish:

> *You awaken cold and trembling. You see the sky gray above through empty branches. You stretch the stiffness from your bones, and turn to look at your horse's body. Your damned horse, whose death has condemned you too to slow death, alone in the wilderness.*

Sounds a lot like the Jay Peterman Catalog on *Seinfeld*, doesn't it?

I don't much like it. Neither do most of those who count; agents, editors, publishers, and importantly, readers. A good practice would be to simply stay away from it.

On the other hand, in the hands of an artist, it *might* work. **Albert Camus'** *The Fall* is an example. And you tell yourself, *surely* you can find another, so you get in your car and head into the city, your mouth dry, your head aching. You stare at the passersby and... oh never mind. The cheese is making its appearance.

Third-Person

Third-person narrative ranks with first-person as the voice of choice. And just as with first-person, there are variations on it. Thoughts and emotions derive from one character's perspective. Not an actual, participating narrator, but as if the narrator is observing the characters. The functional pronouns are "he," "she," "him," and "her," rather than "I" and "me." This is the form in which most fiction is written.

There can be one or more character perspectives, allowing great flexibility.

Third-Person Subjective

Third-person subjective, as the term implies, invokes subjectivity for the viewpoint character. The emotions and thoughts of the viewpoint character may be shown. There may be multiple viewpoint characters, almost without limit. This allows baskets full of writer freedom, but also is the source of many viewpoint errors, simply by volume of shifts.

Stephen King is perhaps the master of using third-person subjective for a large cast of characters. *'Salem's Lot*, for example, engages men, women, children, villains, and monsters—lots of monsters—to bring small-town Maine to life. And death. And undeath. King somehow keeps it all afloat.

Third-Person Limited

Third-person limited describes third-person subjective when scenes are limited to a single viewpoint character throughout the story. All the thoughts, observations, emotions are experienced through that person.

Having read **Dashiell Hammett's** *The Maltese Falcon* some years ago, I thought I'd use it here as a great example of the craft of narration in first-person. I plucked it from my bookshelf to study a few passages.

Surprise! It's in third-person limited.

That still made it ideal as an example to illustrate POV. Maybe even more so. When you read the book, it feels as if it's narrated by Sam Spade as he prowls the streets of San Francisco, piecing together the motives and machinations of a rogue's gallery of unseemly sorts. The point of view is so skillfully done, it took up residence in my memory as a first-person tale.

A Farewell to Arms, by **Ernest Hemingway**, employs a literary approach to third-person limited, following a wounded American volunteer's romance with a nurse in World War I Italy.

Trumbo's Third-Person Limited Experiment

Imagine carrying third-person limited to the extreme. Imagine the viewpoint character with almost no way of experiencing the world around him, and no way of communicating with the world. Imagine the world is completely dark, because you have no eyes. No sound, because your hearing is destroyed. No smell, no taste, no voice… because the lower half of your face is gone. No arms, no legs. Imagine you're merely a torso with a mind.

Impossible to write, isn't it?

No.

Dalton Trumbo accomplished this feat brilliantly in his novel of World War I, *Johnny Got His Gun*. The novel's lone viewpoint character, Joe, has been reduced to existence as a torso with a mind, and the entire novel takes place after he awakens in a hospital bed in this horrifying condition.

> *Calm down he said to himself calm down because you haven't proved anything yet. You may have this thing doped out all wrong. Maybe the things you've assumed are all wrong. If they are then you've got to make a whole new set of assumptions so don't get so cocky. Just calm down and lie back and count five more visits. He dozed*

*a little and thought of a lot of things but
always on the blackboard in his mind he
kept the number two or three or whatever
it was and finally the fifth visit came with
the nurse's feet vibrating on the floor and
her hands on him and the bed.*

Trumbo employs stream-of-consciousness prose
to relay Joe's juggernaut of thoughts, a choice
which reinforces the extreme, almost
claustrophobic, confines of his viewpoint.

Third-Person Objective

Sometimes also called **third-person dramatic**,
third-person objective mode is the "fly on the
wall" or "camera-eye" point of view. No
emotions or thoughts are imparted to the
characters. Literary novels employ this more
than other genres, and even they don't employ it
so much these days.

A strength of third-person objective is that the
view remains unbiased and unfiltered, and
perhaps therefore more honest. The reader
arrives at the meaning of the actions. Some
writers prefer this, as it lets actions speak for
themselves.

In contrast, first-person and third-person
subjective, even though they may communicate
the thoughts, emotions, and motivations of
characters, are not necessarily communicating

honesty. This is because we are often not honest with ourselves, in thought and action. Suppose your third-person subjective protagonist, Sheriff Maddox, is fuming about the nosey reporter that keeps showing up unannounced. You can describe this in his guarded thoughts, but maybe that's not what he's really mad about. Maybe he's mad that his marriage is breaking down and he just doesn't realize it yet. In objective viewpoint, on the other hand, you don't relay Maddox's inner thoughts. You relay only what he does or says.

The camera is a good analogy. A movie camera can only capture what it sees. It can follow a character or characters but can't read thoughts or feel emotions. It makes no assumptions or deductions, but leaves those things to the reader. It records the reactions of the characters to get those things across.

Third-Person Omniscient

Third-person omniscient is frequently confused with objective, but the two are clearly different animals. The omniscient perspective is all-seeing, all-knowing. This can be effective in works of epic scale. In other words, if your novel of World War I involves all the nations drawn into the conflict, you can jump from a scene in which **Kaiser Wilhelm** fires an admiral for sinking the *Lusitania,* to a scene in which

Woodrow Wilson ponders his response to the sinking of the ship.

Omniscient viewpoint can have either subjective or objective viewpoints within the framework. It can follow individual characters closely, and it can also pull back and comment on the proceedings as if from an omniscient observer. It can enter the mind of a grasshopper in the garden with the human characters. It can jump forward or backward in time.

As you might imagine, the tremendous freedom of this mode is also its greatest weakness.

A good example of omniscient is **Alistair MacLean's** first novel, *HMS Ulysses*. MacLean used this mode to capture the complex workings of a warship, rather successfully, although the quick shifts in viewpoint are at times confusing. The narrative moves from one character to another in subjective voice, often within the same scene, and sometimes withdraws to a truly omniscient viewpoint, describing the ferocity of battle or weather as from afar.

Multiple Third-Person Subjective vs. Third-Person Omniscient

Ah, this is where it gets dicey, and there seems to much debate as to how to actually draw the distinction. If omniscient allows access to all characters' minds, isn't that really just the same as having more than one third-person subjective character?

Not quite. The difference is that, in true omniscience, you could be in one character's POV in one paragraph, another's in the next paragraph, and another's in the next. That would get quite confusing in a hurry. Also, omniscience allows for the pull-back camera view.

Limiting a scene or chapter to a single third-person character, and then moving to the next character in the next scene, and so on, constitutes a string of third-person subjective modes. Not as much freedom, but much easier to handle.

Third-Person "Deep"

Traditionally, getting really down inside the psyche of a character lay in the province of the first- person. You could say exactly what the character thought or felt, unfiltered, because you lurked inside the mind of the narrator, hearing her voice. Your standard, garden-variety third-person POV simply couldn't get quite you that deep, because you watched that person, rather than creepily walked around in his skin.

But over time, third-person evolved.

"Deep POV" is point of view taken to another, more intimate level, deep into the thoughts and emotions of the viewpoint character. It eliminates "he thought", "she felt", "he wondered", "she guessed," and the like.

The differences can be subtle. Take for example the following passage, written in a conventional third-person subjective POV:

> *Boothe crept closer. He could see Lincoln now, just a few feet away, sitting there, Mary at his side.*
>
> *He hated the bastard, but wondered if he could go through with it.*

That's pretty up-close-and-personal. You're right there with **John Wilkes Boothe** as he creeps closer to murder, destiny, and infamy.

Now consider the same passage rewritten a bit deeper within the viewpoint character's POV:

> *Boothe crept closer. Lincoln sat there, just a few feet away, Mary at his side.*
>
> *He hesitated. I hate the bastard. But can I go through with it?*

Now you're experiencing the scene unfolding, and not just hearing Boothe's thoughts; you're suddenly *in* Boothe's thoughts. The change is minor; the change is subtle. But it's there, and the level of immediacy is ratcheted up a notch.

21

Third-Person Plural

Much like first-person plural substitutes the collective "we" for the singular "I", **third-person plural** substitutes "they" for "he," "she," and "it." And much like first-person plural, it should only be used with great reservation. Consider:

They talked about the weather and sports, and they gave up. They couldn't get along with anyone and simply gave up. So they ignored their nagging inner voices and settled into sad, quiet lives.

Writing about "they" can sound a little preachy or pretentious, intentionally or not, and come off like a lecture. Which is fine if your goal is to preach and not get published, or read.

PART II

Writing in Viewpoint

Ken Pelham

Choosing Point of View

Okay, now you've got a bucket full of viewpoint options at your disposal. Which one do you use? Can you use more than one? Should you?

The most important question you can ask is: What works best for the story you want to tell? Remember the examples used to illustrate the different techniques. **Arthur Conan Doyle** built his wonderful, enigmatic super-sleuth, Sherlock Holmes, with all those amazing powers of deduction. Doyle selected the POV carefully. He didn't want you inside Holmes' head. Holmes is an enigma precisely because we can't fully see that scary-bright brain working, except through the witness of stalwart Doctor Watson.

Study your genre! If you write romance, pore over romance novels and see which viewpoints are employed. You're on your own here, by the way.

Don't rule out any of the available viewpoint modes when considering how to tell your story. That said, there seem to be some time-tested popular choices among genres. Keep in mind that writing in the past tense is by far the most accepted method; if you choose to write in the present tense, the story will steer the tone into a completely different territory.

Some novel categories, with attendant broad, over-arching suggestions for viewpoint choice are:

Literary or experimental fiction... first-person, third-person subjective, third-person objective. Omniscient might work, too.

Mysteries... often told in first-person or third-person limited. This allows the writer to keep the identity of the evil-doers secret, and allows the protagonist (and the reader) to suspect anyone and everyone. The classic whodunit almost always restricts the viewpoint characters to just one.

Thrillers & Horror... multiple third-person subjective allows the writer to build suspense by having multiple characters pursuing their own ends. A disadvantage is that it's harder to keep a broad number of suspects. If you don't care if the reader knows who the bad guys are, it's not a problem. The bad guy is quite often a viewpoint character.

Science Fiction... first- or third-person subjective. In **Margaret Atwood's** *The Handmaid's Tale*, Offred's story is told in first-person narrative. Atwood made the best choice; first-person lets us get close to Offred's dissatisfaction and anger at the state of her world, and lets her slowly come to realize that other things are afoot. It's an awakening of one woman's thoughts, not watered down with the aims of others around her. Authors of longer SF works seem to employ multiple third-person.

Fantasy... because a lot of fantasy novels run considerably longer than most other genres, multiple third-person takes a front seat. The epic nature of these also lends them well to an omniscient narrative, as in *The Lord of the Rings*.

Romance... multiple third-person subjective seems to be a mode of favor, as it allows the writer to build a level of intimacy within multiple characters (although probably focusing on the two that make up the couple).

In short stories and novellas of any genre, the writer might be best served by sticking to first-person or third-person limited.

Viewpoint in Nonfiction

We've looked at fictional viewpoint thus far, but the same rules apply to nonfiction, particularly that of the "creative" variety. Creative nonfiction and the "nonfiction novel" introduced viewpoint much more.

Now if you're looking to write academic or technical nonfiction, say for textbooks, the dictates of the field may not let you stray into subjective viewpoint land at all. By convention, these works are detached and dispassionate.

That's how you get taken seriously—although not necessarily read—in those fields. Subjective character viewpoint doesn't typically apply. Just the opposite applies, and objectivity, or at least the appearance thereof, is the standard.

Objective omniscient rules the day, and is indeed perhaps preferred in a history. Omniscient allows the author to describe events taking place simultaneously all over the world. To illustrate, a history of World War I might jump from **Csar Nicholas II's** drawing room to **Archduke Ferdinand's** fateful carriage ride through Sarajevo. The meaning of events and the timing gathers weight when they're seen from broad perspectives.

Memoirs and autobiographies are obviously told in first-person, unless the author gets cute and refers to himself in the third-person. Fine examples are *Night,* by **Elie Wiesel**, and *Rocket Boys,* by **Homer Hickam**.

Some creative nonfiction books are in first- *and* third-person. In **John Berendt's** account of high-society sex and murder in Savannah, *Midnight in the Garden of Good and Evil*, the majority of scenes are in Berendt's own first-person narration, while other parts are told in first-person by other characters.

Do Not Disturb...

You've got a grip on the basics of viewpoint types and terminology. You've deduced what might work best for your story. Now for the nitty-gritty, the real lessons in viewpoint.

Remember: the reader stays hooked when not disturbed. A narrative should be fluid and seamless in order to avoid disturbing the reader. Every time point of view changes, the reader is disturbed just a little.

What a Character Knows (or Doesn't)

The key to mastering a subjective viewpoint is understanding what a character can and can't know. This is not always readily apparent. You must put yourself—the writer—in the character's shoes and experience things she can experience. Notice I said "experience," and not "see." Point of view doesn't mean strictly the visual. All the senses contribute to point of view. Furthermore, thinking and feeling contribute to point of view. If the viewpoint character didn't experience it, it didn't happen and you can't write it. Out of sight, out of mind...

In anything other than objective viewpoint, you have to understand what a character can and can't see, hear, smell, taste, sense, intuit, and think.

Consider the following passage:

> *General Lee reined in his horse, and surveyed Fredericksburg across the river. Dawn was breaking cold and gray, the fog hiding God only knew what. Nearby, a sentry leaned against an oak, dozing, his head nodding. Lee snapped a thin branch off the tree and swatted the man. "Damn you, soldier! Burnside could have slipped his whole army across the river. I won't lose this war because you can't keep your eyes open."*

> *The soldier collected himself. He saluted, picked up his gun, and turned away to face Fredericksburg. A scowl darkened his face and he muttered under his breath.*

What's wrong here? Spot the POV problem?

It went swimmingly. At least until the last sentence.

General Lee is the third-person subjective viewpoint character. That's established at the start, and our viewpoint is his. Imagine seeing through his eyes. When the slacker sentry turns his back to Lee, we're asked to understand that "a scowl darkened his face." Maybe it did. How do *we* know, if General Lee doesn't know? Is

Lee so brilliant he just knows? Nope. Maybe he saw the soldier's face reflected in a mirror. If so, the author had better say so.

Now of course I overstate the case, "out of sight, out of mind" a trifle. You don't necessarily have to see everything. Lee might hear the soldier muttering, and might imagine the scowl. But the author needs to frame it that way. One might write:

> *The soldier turned away and muttered something under his breath.*
>
> *Lee grimaced, realizing he'd not made his point, and figured he'd produced an unhappy, scowling infantryman, and swatted the man again. "What's that, soldier?"*

Lee "knew" the man was scowling, but it's framed as an assumption, not as something that happened that he did not in fact witness.

Dialogue

Always start a new paragraph whenever there's a dialogue switch from one character to another. This shouldn't even have to be said. We learned it in middle school. "Just do it," the teacher barked. He didn't explain the reasoning behind his command.

31

It's all about POV. It gives order, it gives sequence. It allows the reader to follow easily.

Consider:

> *"Where you headed?" Caldwell asked. "Downtown?" Louise shrugged. "Yeah. Maybe. I'll figure it out on my way."*

Horrific writing, that. We spot it instantly. That middle school English teacher would have scored it F-, which is as low a grade as you can get. And I would have deserved it.

Here's a weak attempt at improvement:

> *"Where you headed?" Caldwell asked. Downtown?" Louise shrugged.*
>
> *"Yeah. Maybe. I'll figure it out on my way."*

At least the dialogue is now separated into different paragraphs. But it could be much better. The problem is that we're following Caldwell's action (a snippet of dialogue), and then Louise shrugged. In the same paragraph. While that may be legal in most states and parts of Idaho, it mistakenly still jams Louise's action (a shrug) into Caldwell's, then correctly drops her follow-up action (dialogue) to the next paragraph. This error is quite common, and often creeps into publication. In stream-of-consciousness prose it actually works, but in most other styles, it tends to make a decided *clunk.*

> *"Where you headed?" Caldwell asked.*
> *"Downtown?"*

> *Louise shrugged. "Yeah. Maybe. I'll figure*
> *it out on my way."*

Now everything is ordered properly and easy to consume in bite-size chunks without even a minimal buttering of confusion.

How a Character Sees Others

Writers are often told they need to go into great detail when describing characters. I don't necessarily agree with that school of thought, and prefer to give only the sketchiest descriptions of individuals, and let the reader's imagination fill in the details. Either way, the writer must relate that description sensibly, telling it just as the viewpoint character would see someone.

Suppose I'm writing about a married couple, and churn out this gem:

> *I turned to look at Lisa. My wife had long*
> *beautiful hair and dark, luminous eyes.*

Problem: My viewpoint character just now realized what his wife looks like? This sort of information doesn't pop up believably (unless my viewpoint character's blindness has been miraculously cured).

To understand this in real life, imagine going to a party. When I arrive I tell the hostess, "This is my wife. She has long beautiful hair and dark, luminous eyes." Okay, you get that I married a babe, but must I beat you over the head with it (her)?

Realizing my clumsiness, in the revision, I handle it a little better:

> *I turned to look at Lisa. My wife was still beautiful after twenty years of marriage, her hair long and lustrous, her eyes dark and luminous.*

Problem: The narrator would not suddenly notice looks that haven't changed in twenty years. Her characteristics should have already been established. If she'd dyed her hair blond or put on a lot of makeup or transformed into a wolf, *that* would warrant noticing.

This kind of revelation *might* work if I'm trying to establish that POV Guy is seeing her as if for the first time, having forgotten why he loved her. Use with caution and skill.

Seeing One's Self

Frequent mistakes appear when the writer is trying to describe the viewpoint character. You want to let your readers know what your protagonist, Saunders, looks like. So you introduce him this way:

Saunders slipped into an open door and eased it shut behind him. He took a deep breath and ran his fingers through his jet-black hair, trying to steady his nerves.

Problem: Viewpoint characters don't think about their own looks or voices. Except for the exceptionally vain amongst us, we don't traipse around thinking about the color of our hair. Or that we have big ears. Or a W.C. Fields nose. Only if the character were trying to somehow hide his appearance or traits would he be thinking about them.

Some readers and writers, of course, love detailed descriptions of each character that waltzes into the story. They love reading that the hero has a gap-toothed grin, and a hairy mole on his forehead. Unless it's integral to something in the plot (such as a twist based on misidentification of a suspect), I don't. Fleeting descriptions satisfy me as a reader, and my imagination lets the character be what he or she should look like. Long descriptions force an image that may not sit well. But that's a personal preference.

If you *must* describe the viewpoint character, do it through the observations of a non-viewpoint character:

> *Lisa rubbed Saunders' head, and laughed.*
> *"You think your gorgeous jet-black hair is*
> *going to get you into* that *club? Ha!"*

Another way to portray a viewpoint character's description is to have him studying himself in a mirror, a reflection in a pool, a window pane, or something similar. Maybe watching a video of himself, or studying his wedding photo and thinking about how much they've both changed in the intervening years.

In my novel, *Brigands Key*, I introduce a character with this:

> *Gerald Hammond stubbed his cigarette,*
> *sprayed a blast of freshener into his*
> *mouth, and wondered why he bothered.*
> *Everyone in Brigands Key knew he*
> *sneaked a smoke now and then. He'd been*
> *the only doctor in town worth a flip in*
> *twenty years and no one was going to run*
> *him out on account of smoking, so long as*
> *he had the decency to not cough smoke*
> *into their faces.*

> *He cupped his hand in front of his mouth*
> *and blew. Not bad. He stretched his back,*
> *relishing its satisfying pops, and went to*
> *the bathroom adjoining his office and*
> *studied his reflection in the mirror. A*
> *slight paunch, only a few wrinkles, and the*
> *wispy brown hair atop his head had not*
> *given up the struggle. Yet.*

Information about Hammond's appearance and personality is delivered through his actions, such as sneaking a smoke and trying to mask it, and his subsequent musing over it. The gimmick of checking himself out in the mirror helps round him out with a few physical details. However, be careful not to go to this well too often, as it will indeed come off like a gimmick.

Mind-Readers

Unless your story actually *is* about mind-readers, be careful not to make your characters mind-readers. Out of sight, out of mind. The viewpoint character doesn't know what someone else is thinking. Don't make assumptions; that's the reader's job. Let the details tell the story, and let the reader make those informed assumptions and educated guesses.

Suppose I take another stab at my novel about Narrator Neil and his wife Lisa. I write:

> *I turned to look at Lisa. She was thinking about our argument last night.*

Problem: I, the godlike writer, know what Lisa's thinking. But the narrator *doesn't* (unless he's psychic).

Aghast, I realize my great error and make it a little better:

> *I turned to look at Lisa. She seemed to be deep in thought. Maybe about last night. I hoped like hell it wasn't.*

The narrator notes that Lisa *seemed* to be deep in thought. He doesn't *know* it, and it's not related as fact. It's acceptable and doesn't violate viewpoint. However, it's not particularly well done, in that there's no real emotion, action, or detail to move the story forward.

I revise, and make it better still:

> *I turned to look at Lisa.*

> *She stared into her cup, not saying a word. Lines creased her forehead.*

> *I hoped like hell this wasn't about last night.*

Now we're getting somewhere. In this revision, speculations such as "Lisa seemed" are replaced by actions, as observed by the viewpoint character. The narrator and reader see that Lisa is probably deep in thought—and probably pissed—without being told. I would quietly exit the room if I were the narrator.

Later, I write:

> *I turned to look at Lisa.*

> *She stared into her empty coffee cup.*

Problem: Unless the narrator has witnessed her pouring it out on the floor, how does he know her coffee cup is empty? Because she's not taking a sip that very moment? If it's not empty, how does he know it's got coffee in it, and not brandy or arsenic, or both (which might make a good plot twist)? Answer is, he doesn't. The only way this passage would be in consistent viewpoint would be if the narrator came over, peered over her shoulder into the cup, saw that it was empty, and asked if it had coffee in it before. And that would be about as clumsy as prose can get.

Show, Don't Tell

The "show, don't tell" rule is essential to creative writing. You've heard it a million times, and for good reason; it brings prose to life. A side benefit is that it actually helps the writer avoid viewpoint errors. Consider the following:

Jake stared at Marcie, and felt his heart thudding in his chest. She was mad.

Problem: The writer reports through Jake that Marcie was mad. Unless it has been established in previous paragraphs, Jake doesn't really know she's mad. Maybe she's just deep in thought, which, if true, hasn't been effectively illustrated. Or maybe she applied her makeup badly and it ended up like warpaint.

Don't say she's mad. *Show it.*

> *Jake stared at Marcie, and felt his heart thudding in his chest.*
>
> *Her eyes narrowed, and redness crept into her cheeks. "You... you damned..." She snatched the ashtray off the table and hurled it at his face.*

Viewpoint is consistent, plus the passive voice—"was mad"—is replaced by active description. We no longer suppose she's mad. She demonstrates it.

Novice writers are tempted to add modifiers and extra description. In the example above, imagine that the author, feeling the urge to expound, writes a slightly different version:

> *Jake stared at Marcie, and felt his heart thudding in his chest.*
>
> *Her eyes narrowed, and red crept hotly into her cheeks. "You... you damned... " She snatched the ashtray off the table and hurled it at his face.*

Problem: Again, we're experiencing this scene through Jake's viewpoint. He sees (and therefore knows) her eyes are narrowing... *(check!)*... can see redness creeping into her face... *(check!)*... but how does he know it's doing so "hotly?" *(Clunk! Dammit.)* Does he produce a thermometer and sample her temperature? Extra detail can be good, but not if it violates point of view.

Viewpoint Changes in Third-Person

Avoiding viewpoint changes helps avoid viewpoint errors. However, if you do switch, simplify and make the switch obvious.

A good overall strategy is limiting the number of changes. One viewpoint character should have a plurality of scenes (in novels).

In short stories, there's little need or reason to switch viewpoint characters, although it *can* be done. Stick with one viewpoint character the whole way through.

When changing viewpoint characters, identify the new POV character in the *first* sentence, if not the first word. I've read stories in which the author switched the viewpoint character without immediately identifying the new viewpoint character. After a lengthy paragraph or two, the new POV was finally mentioned. You have to go back and read it again for it to make sense. How this could get by an editor is beyond me, but it does.

Using only one viewpoint per scene makes for a good practice. In omniscient, you can bounce around, but it's not the best idea ever and is a weakness of the omniscient mode. In long scenes with lots going on simultaneously (such as in a battle), I confess to having made switches within the scene, being careful to make the switch immediately apparent.

Head-Hoppers

Head-hopping is pretty much what it sounds like, quantum leaps within a scene from one character's viewpoint to another's, and then maybe to someone else's, and then maybe back to the first character's. Don't do it. It's confusing. The writer might claim, "Ah, but I'm in omniscient mode now. Therefore, I can and shall." True, that's omniscient. That doesn't make it right.

I've read a few manuscripts in which the head-hopping goes overboard, with the result that I soon had no idea which character was doing what.

If you change viewpoints within a scene, be careful and be obvious. There's nothing wrong with being obvious. And have a good reason to make the shift.

In one scene of my novel, *Place of Fear*, I begin in the viewpoint of Linda Stein. She's on watch late at night, and hearing stealthy sounds in the surrounding rainforest. Carson Grant is dozing nearby. Linda wakes him, tells him what she's heard. He urges her to retire for the night and he'll take over her watch. As she goes to her tent, viewpoint shifts to him. Now *he* starts hearing things in the forest. Shifting viewpoint in mid-scene allowed me to highlight the claustrophobic feel of the vast rainforest, as Linda sees it, and illuminate Grant's initial smug skepticism and subsequent alarm. I tried writing this scene entirely in her viewpoint, and also entirely in Grant's, but splitting the scene between them seemed to be the most effective, creating a bit of levity just before all hell breaks loose. Point is, have a good reason.

Be True to the Character

In first-person or in third-person subjective, the narrative voice must be true to the POV character, and *sound* like that character.

In first-person this is almost self-evident. Consider the classic example of **Mark Twain's** *Huckleberry Finn*, in which the novel is told entirely in Huck's first-person narrative:

> *The widow she cried over me, and called me a poor lost lamb, and she called me a lot of other names, too, but she never meant no harm by it. She put me in them new clothes again, and I couldn't do nothing but sweat and sweat, and feel all cramped up. Well, then, the old thing commenced again. The widow rung a bell*

43

*for supper, and you had to come to time.
When you got to the table you couldn't go
right to eating, but you had to wait for the
widow to tuck down her head and grumble
a little over the victuals, though there
warn't really anything the matter with
them, --that is, nothing only everything
was cooked by itself. In a barrel of odds
and ends it is different; things get mixed
up, and the juice kind of swaps around,
and the things go better.*

The written voice is authentic to Huck's spoken
voice, he being the backwoods scamp not at all
comfortable amongst the widow's finery and
good manners (even though he seems to
understand good food better than her).

In contrast, Twain's first-person narrator in *A
Connecticut Yankee in King Arthur's Court* is a
highly educated engineer of the 19th-century,
transplanted into 6th-century Arthurian England:

*Inherited ideas are a curious thing, and
interesting to observe and examine. I had
mine, the king and his people had theirs.
In both cases they flowed in ruts worn
deep by time and habit, and the man who
should have proposed to divert them by
reason and argument would have had a
long contract on his hands.*

Same author, same style, same incisive wit... and completely different voices for the two narratives.

That use of voice is clear in the first-person, but it also applies to the third-person subjective narrative. Suppose you're writing about a good ole boy, Jimbo, who's about to get into some unseemly business or other in the barn down the road a piece from Pete's County-Line Bar and Grill:

> *Jimbo glanced at his watch. Midnight. He sat in his pickup, thinking what a damn fine mess he'd got himself into. He had to go inside and fetch them pictures before anybody else saw them. Trouble was, he was flat-out scared. The barn door leaned to one side, open before him, the perspective awry, reminiscent of an M.C. Escher drawing.*

Yikes. This works fine, up until the last sentence. Then it does a face-plant.

The problem is, we've clearly established Jimbo's character, right down to the narrative saying "fetch them pictures" and "trouble was, he was flat-out scared." That viewpoint voice is true to his character, even if he doesn't say it out loud. Then we ruin it by describing a listing barn door as having "the perspective awry, reminiscent of an M.C. Escher drawing." Everything about that last sentence screams

Greenwich Village art gallery and wine crowd. Sure, it's *possible* in some alternate universe that Jimbo absorbs *The New Yorker* every night, but unless you're going for comedy gold, or unless Jimbo is an elite undercover agent, as equally comfortable in Hawg Waller, Alabama as he is in a Manhattan bistro, it doesn't work.

In my short story, "The Wreck of the Edinburgh Kate," set in 1890, the third-person narrative takes a rather formal, high-sounding tone, befitting an educated Bostonian of the 19th-century. A modern cadence and inflection would have flopped.

> *The plunder reached frightful proportion in those days, but the tower and its great beacon had become the savior of mariners, and ships no longer ran aground in the shallows about the island, and that source of easy wealth had vanished. But the stories and the lust still ran in these men's veins. The unlikely wreckage today had brought it swiftly to the surface.*

Likewise, bandying about phrases like "frightful proportion" won't work if you're writing a third-person about a 21st-century inner city kid.

Mixing and Matching Viewpoints

Viewpoint doesn't necessarily have to be the same throughout the story, as long as it's consistent within any given scene. Shifts can occur within the framework if you know the limiting rules of each. You might do a chapter in first-person as narrated by Character Jimbo, do the next chapter in first-person as related by his court-appointed attorney, and the next chapter in first-person as told by hard-ass ATF Agent Willy Wilson.

But mixing and matching viewpoints can go beyond multiple first-person. With care and with a little experience in the crafting of viewpoint, you might employ first-person with third-person in various scenes.

Douglas Preston and **Lincoln Child** employ a particularly clever mixing of viewpoints in their Special Agent Pendergast series. Overall, the novels have multiple third-person subjective points of view. You know what Corrie or D'Agosta or Smithback are thinking at all times. But the authors have developed main protagonist Pendergast as an enigmatic sort, uncomfortable with intimacy, guarded of his privacy, and difficult to understand. To further this image of him, they subtly shift from subjective to objective when the scene is following him. The illusion is sustained and the shift fits his personality like a glove.

In my novel, *Brigands Key*, I chose to tell the great bulk of the story in third-person subjective with multiple viewpoint characters. The plot involves the discovery of a nude body in an undersea cave off the coast of Florida. The body's time of death confounds both the local and national investigators. The body's discovery triggers a string of competing agendas among the local citizenry, so the tale naturally lent itself to multiple viewpoint characters.

Many sequences within the novel step up briefly into deep POV, allowing greater emphasis on certain moments, heightening the tension.

Plot-wise, I needed to disseminate inside information to the bigger world outside the insular island town of Brigands Key. I did so by writing a good chunk of the thoughts of character Charley Fawcett, an 18-year old misfit, in the form of his blog. Charley spills his inner thoughts anonymously this way, helping move the story incidents along. Additionally, key background is uncovered in the form of Captain Remarque's memoir, which performs the vital service of at last illuminating and explaining the central mystery of the ageless body.

The blog passages of Charley, and the memoir of Remarque are therefore in the first-person. As mentioned earlier this is termed an epistolary narrative or as if the narrative character had actually written it in the form of documents.

A sample of Charley's blog:

So I go to work this morning like a good little proletarian. Roscoe's not there again. That's two days. Yippee, right? No, Roscoe's always there. But not now. Dude up and ran off, no word, no nothing. The hell am I supposed to do? Can't take the boat out for him... I'd sink it before I cleared the channel. I checked Roscoe's house five times to see if he's around. Nope. When I get back home this morning, the Old Man is waiting. Crap, he's going to lay into me for quitting a good-paying job, which I didn't, but the Old Man has his mind made up that I'm worthless. And what does he do? Nothing. Looks at me, growls, goes back to bed. Not feeling good. Man, I catch a break. A hangover can be a true friend.

About a third of the way through the novel, as the mystery deepens and the various aims of the characters take shape, I inserted a single brief scene told in omniscient point of view. This scene describes shifts in atmospheric conditions far out in the Gulf of Mexico, elemental changes which spur the rapid development of an unnamed storm into the monster that will become Hurricane Celeste. Up until that point the brewing weather is only mentioned in passing in the third-person musings of a couple of characters.

I debated this at length as drafts of the novel progressed, fearing that mixing of omniscient with first- and third-person narratives might disrupt the feel and pace. In the end, it just felt right, and I'm glad I kept it, as it foreshadowed the looming crisis. I've mentioned this viewpoint change to a number of editors and readers. None felt that it had jarred them out of the story, and in fact they had scarcely even noticed the change, so I feel pretty confident that it was successful.

When we shift gears to Captain Remarque's memoir, at one stage he recounts the story told him by a spy. The story is told to Remarque in the first-person, and he relates it that way. In other words, it's a nested first-person narrative within another first-person narrative that is in itself a nested into the overall third-person structure of the novel.

Therefore, the novel moves along on the freighted wheels of first-person multiple, nested first-person, multiple third-person, and omniscient points of view. Readers and reviewers have remarked that a favorite feature is Charley's self-indulgent blog, and another reader tells me that she was swept up in Captain Remarque's memoir, which only appears late in the book.

As stated earlier, consistency in viewpoint is vital. However, characters can and should grow in some manner over the course of the story.

Sometimes it's a little, sometimes it's a lot. But they, just like the rest of us, change over time. Viewpoint, correctly handled, accommodates that change.

In *Brigands Key*, early in the novel, Dr. Carson Grant is a true outsider in this untrusting little town. To Jerry Hammond, the town's only physician and medical examiner, and Randy Sanborn, the Chief of Police, Carson Grant is just "Grant." They aren't his friends and don't care to be, and this is how he's referred to in their third-person narratives.

To Charley Fawcett, a bright kid, Grant represents someone to admire, the super-smart outsider, so Charley largely thinks of him as "Doctor Grant."

To Kyoko Nakamura, a pathologist with the Center for Disease Control, and an unwelcome outsider like Grant, he is also just "Grant." For a while anyway. After they become intimate, her third-person scenes begin to refer to him as "Carson."

Characters change. That's what story is all about, after all. When they do change, the way characters relate their feelings also changes. To keep the language of their viewpoints consistent, their labels for other characters might have to change.

Closing Arguments...

Point of view is the source of many errors (and rejection slips). The mistakes can be glaring or subtle; neither kind does your manuscript any favors. The subtle ones get frequently missed, even by experienced writers, agents, and editors. And, as editorial budgets shrink, the frequency of those misses seems to be increasing, so you can't rely on an editor to root them out. Errors surface sometimes in the works of authors on the bestseller lists. They might not ruin everything, but the writing would be stronger without them. As mentioned at the start of this little book, they go *clunk*.

The bad POV mistakes can keep you from getting published, or if you're self-publishing, keep you from getting repeat readers and building a fan base.

Ultimately, in the hands of an artist, all rules can be bent and broken. But not before they are known inside and out, and mastered.

To manage and master viewpoint, do the following:

- Know and understand the different modes of viewpoint.

- Study POV in the next few books or stories you read.

- Study how POV is handled successfully in the genre you write.

- Select the mode that best suits the story you want to tell.

- Stay in the active voice.

- Show, don't tell.

- Keep it simple.

- Avoid head-hopping within a scene.

- Reread your manuscript, and place yourself in the narrator's POV. Ask yourself: can I see, hear, think, intuit, or somehow experience what the POV narrator is experiencing?

- Keep the narrative voice true to the POV character.

- Mix and match viewpoint modes only after you've gotten a feel for each.

All writers experiment with how best to write a first draft, and how best to revise the successive drafts. Some knock out a first draft in as great a rush of creation as they can muster, all sound and fury, with nary a thought as to how it reads. Others write a paragraph of a first draft and then meticulously rewrite and polish it several times before moving on to the next paragraph. Most, I suspect, are somewhere in between those two extremes. There's no right or wrong way. My advice, and my approach, is to choose POV wisely and carefully before setting pen to paper or electron to phosphor. Be *aware* of viewpoint in your first draft, but don't worry too much about errors in a first (or even second) draft. There's plenty of time to polish it later.

Understanding viewpoint is critical.

Now then. Get back to work. All of you. Get those viewpoints fixed, and best of luck in everything you write!

Also available online:

Treacherous Bastards: Stories of Suspense, Deceit, and Skullduggery...
A collection of three stories in the Hitchcock tradition, including one about the little island of Brigands Key.

A Double Shot of Fright: Two Tales of Terror...
Two chilling short stories guaranteed to cause loss of sleep.

Tales of Old Brigands Key...
Three short stories about the strange little island and its somewhat unsavory past.

Ken is a member of Florida Writers Association and International Thriller Writers. Visit him at **www.kenpelham.com** for updates on his work, and musings on suspense fiction.

Made in the USA
Monee, IL
18 October 2020

45418164R00038

Ken Pelham

Thanks for reading, and I hope you've found this book helpful. If so, it'll be much appreciated if you could post a review online.

For a companion how-to manual on keeping readers on the edges of their seats, please check out ***Great Danger: A Writer's Guide to Building Suspense***, available online.

Thanks!
--kp

About the Author...

Ken Pelham lives and writes in Maitland, Florida. His thriller, **Brigands Key**, won first place in the Florida Writers Association's Royal Palm Literary Awards and was published in hardcover in 2012 by Cengage/Five Star Mystery. The ebook edition came out in 2013.

Brigands Key is "...a perfect storm of menace... breathtaking!"
--The Florida Weekly

His follow-up novel, **Place of Fear**, also a first place winner of the Royal Palm Literary Award, was published in 2013.

It's none of their business that you have to learn to write. Let them think you were born that way.

--Ernest Hemingway